Curriculum Visions

Jewish synagogue

Studying in a synagogue

Lisa Magloff

Word list

Look out for these words as you go through the book. They are shown using CAPITALS.

ARK The closet-like cabinet in which the Torah scrolls are kept in the synagogue. The name Ark comes from the Hebrew words *Aron HaKodesh*, which means Holy Cabinet.

BAR/BAT MITZVAH The ceremony when a boy or girl reads from the Torah, for the first time, during worship.

BIMAH The raised platform from which the Torah is read during services.

BOOK OF PROPHETS A Jewish holy book that contains the writings of some of the ancient prophets.

COMMANDMENT A law, or rule, given to people by God. Jews believe that God gave them 613 commandments.

HEBREW The language that the Torah is written in. Hebrew was first spoken thousands of years ago. Today, a modern version of Hebrew is spoken in Israel.

HOLOCAUST Refers to a time between 1941 and 1945 when the Nazis killed more than six million Jews throughout Europe. In Hebrew, it is called the *shoah*.

ISRAEL The country that was the ancient homeland of the Jewish people. Modern Israel was founded in 1948 as a homeland for Jews from all over the world.

JEW/JEWISH PEOPLE Any person whose parents are Jewish or who has converted to Judaism.

JUDAISM A religion developed in ancient times which includes belief in one God, and living according to the laws written in the Torah and according to Jewish traditions.

KIPPAH A cap worn by Jewish men as a symbol of respect for God. It is also called a skullcap.

MENORAH A lamp stand with seven branches, which is placed in the sanctuary of the synagogue. It represents a similar lamp which was in the Temple in ancient Jerusalem.

MEZUZAH A small box which contains a copy of a prayer called the Shema, and is attached to doorposts of many Jewish homes and synagogues.

MITZVAH A Hebrew word which means commandments.

NER TAMID A lamp which is kept burning in the sanctuary, near the Ark. The words *ner tamid* mean eternal light.

PARCHMENT A type of paper made from animal skin.

PROPHET A person in ancient times, chosen by God to speak to people on God's behalf, and to convey a message or teaching. A spokesperson for God.

PURIM A Jewish holiday which celebrates the ancient time when a Jewish woman called Esther saved the lives of all the Jews living in Persia. It is also called the Feast of Esther.

RABBI A religious teacher and person authorised to make decisions on issues of Jewish law. The rabbi also performs many of the same functions as a minister such as leading worship, giving sermons and helping people.

ROSH HASHANAH The Jewish New Year. An important Jewish holiday in which each person prays and thinks about how to become a better person in the coming year.

SANCTUARY The part of the synagogue that contains the Ark.

SHABBAT The Jewish Sabbath, or day of rest. It begins at sundown on Friday and ends at sundown on Saturday.

SHEMA One of the most important Jewish prayers. *Shema* is a Hebrew word which means to hear and listen. The prayer has three paragraphs and each one is a short passage from the Torah.

SIDDUR The prayer book used during worship.

STAR OF DAVID A symbol of Judaism, also called the Shield of David. In Hebrew it is called *Magen David*. The star was a symbol of King David, an important ancient Jewish king.

SYNAGOGUE A building used for worship and the centre of the Jewish community.

TALLIT A shawl-like garment worn during morning services, with tzitzit attached to the corners as a reminder of the commandments. A tallit is sometimes called a prayer shawl.

TEFILLIN Leather pouches containing scrolls with passages from the Torah, used to fulfil the commandment to bind the commandments to our hands and between our eyes.

TEN COMMANDMENTS Ten of the most important commandments in the Torah. They are the same in Judaism and in Christianity.

THE TEMPLE A synagogue built in Jerusalem and the centre of the Jewish religion in ancient times. It was destroyed in 586 BCE, rebuilt and then destroyed again in 70 CE.

TORAH The Jewish Bible. The Torah is made up of the first five books of the Old Testament of the Bible. The Torah is the principle Jewish holy book and many Jews believe that it is the direct word of God.

TZEDAKAH A Hebrew word which means righteousness. It refers to money or other types of charity. Giving to charity is an important part of the Jewish religion.

TZITZIT Fringes attached to the corners of garments as a reminder of the commandments.

Contents

Word list 2

What is a synagogue? 4

Inside the synagogue 6

The heart of the synagogue 8

The sanctuary........................ 10

Clothing for worship................. 12

A daily house of worship 14

Shabbat and the Torah 16

A house of learning 18

Celebrations and festivals........ 20

A house of gathering 22

Index..................................... 24

Be considerate!

When visiting a place of worship, remember that it is sacred to believers and so be considerate to their feelings. It doesn't take a lot of effort – just attitude.

An Ark with the doors closed

What is a synagogue?

A synagogue is one building with three different roles.

JUDAISM began thousands of years ago in West Asia, near the modern country of **ISRAEL**. Israel is very special to **JEWISH PEOPLE**. Although **JEWS** live all over the world, it is the land many Jews believe God promised to their ancestors. It is sometimes called "the promised land".

▼ ① **A synagogue is a house of prayer.**

The ancient Jews spoke a language called **HEBREW**, and so many important words, prayers and holy books in Judaism are written in Hebrew. For example, the **SYNAGOGUE** actually has three names in Hebrew. Each name stands for one of the three ways that the synagogue is used.

▼ ② A synagogue is a house of learning.

House of gathering

Beit HaKnesset is the Hebrew word for house of gathering (the word synagogue is actually the Greek translation of *Beit HaKnesset*). The synagogue is called a house of gathering because it is a place for the Jewish community to come together for all types of meetings, celebrations and other community activities.

House of prayer

Beit HaTefillah is the Hebrew word for house of prayer. The synagogue is called a house of prayer because it is where Jews come to worship God (picture ①). Jews also worship at home and by themselves, but worshipping with others is an important part of Judaism.

House of learning

Beit HaMidrash is the Hebrew word for house of learning. The synagogue is a house of learning because it is where Jews come to learn the Hebrew language and to learn about Judaism. In most synagogues, children and adults can take classes in Hebrew, study important Jewish religious books and learn all about Judaism (picture ②).

In the following pages we will learn more about how the synagogue fills each of these three roles.

Weblink: www.CurriculumVisions.com

Inside the synagogue

Almost everything that you will see inside the synagogue has an important meaning in Judaism.

The building

There is no special design for a synagogue building (picture ①) but many of the things you will see inside the synagogue are designed to remind worshippers of a synagogue built thousands of years ago in Jerusalem. This synagogue was called **THE TEMPLE** and it was built by an important Jewish king called King Solomon.

Most synagogues are built with one wall facing Jerusalem as a reminder of the Temple.

Some synagogues are also built with a deliberate design flaw. This is to remind worshippers that only God can create perfection.

In some synagogues, women sit in a separate area for worship, but in many synagogues women and men sit together.

Prayer boxes

If you look closely at some of the doorways in the synagogue you may see a small, colourful box called a **MEZUZAH** (picture ②).

On the outside of the mezuzah you may see a Hebrew letter. This is the letter 'shin' and it is the first

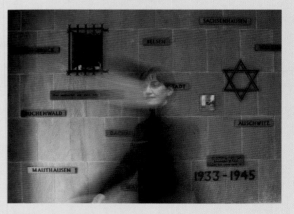

Wall of remembrance

Many synagogues have a HOLOCAUST memorial. This could be a plaque, or a wall of remembrance, dedicated to the six million Jews who died before and during World War II. The memorial also reminds people not to let such tragedies ever happen again.

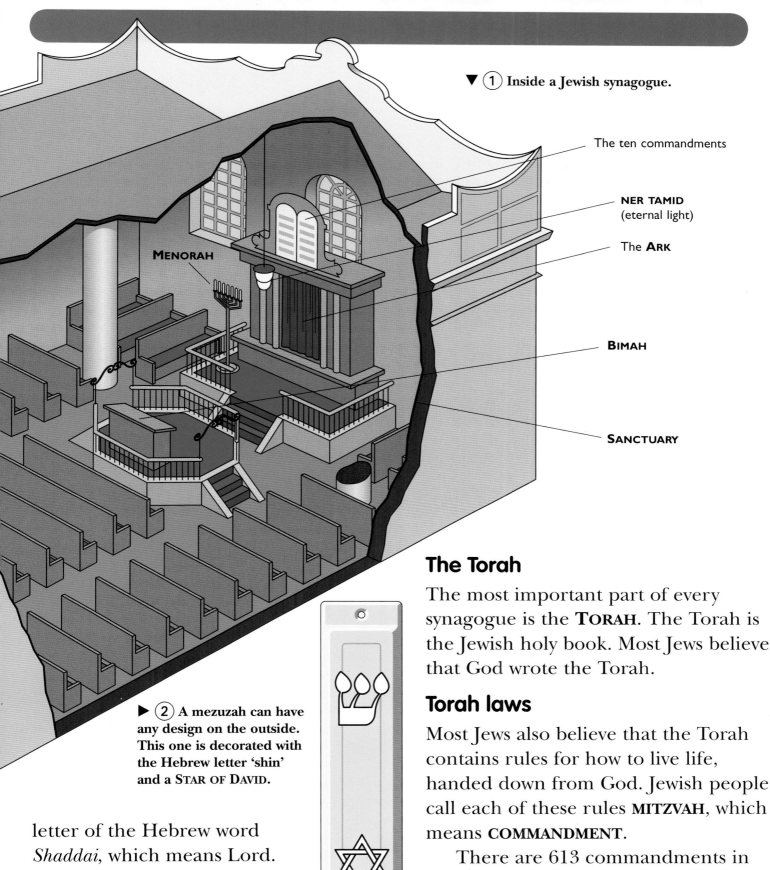

▼ ① Inside a Jewish synagogue.

The ten commandments

NER TAMID
(eternal light)

The **ARK**

MENORAH

BIMAH

SANCTUARY

▶ ② A mezuzah can have any design on the outside. This one is decorated with the Hebrew letter 'shin' and a STAR OF DAVID.

letter of the Hebrew word *Shaddai*, which means Lord. Inside each mezuzah is a little parchment scroll with the words of a special prayer called the **SHEMA** written on it.

The Torah

The most important part of every synagogue is the **TORAH**. The Torah is the Jewish holy book. Most Jews believe that God wrote the Torah.

Torah laws

Most Jews also believe that the Torah contains rules for how to live life, handed down from God. Jewish people call each of these rules **MITZVAH**, which means **COMMANDMENT**.

There are 613 commandments in the Torah. You are probably already familiar with some of the most important commandments – the **TEN COMMANDMENTS**.

7

Weblink: www.CurriculumVisions.com

The heart of the synagogue

The Torah is what makes the synagogue an important place.

The Torah scroll

The **TORAH** contains more than commandments, it also contains stories about God and about people who are important to the Jews. The Torah also contains sayings which show what is important in life, for example, "love your neighbour as yourself."

During some worship services, parts of the Torah are read out loud in the synagogue. When the Torah is read in the synagogue, it is read from a scroll.

A Torah scroll must be written on **PARCHMENT** and it must be written by hand (picture ①). It must not have any mistakes in it, or else it cannot be used.

Torah scrolls are very precious because they contain the word of God.

▶ ① The Torah scroll is held up during worship so everyone can see it.

8

The Ark

The Torah scrolls are kept in a cabinet called the **ARK** (pictures ① and ②). The word Ark is short for the Hebrew words *Aron HaKodesh,* which means Holy Cabinet.

Above and in front of the Ark there is a lamp, called the **NER TAMID** (pictures ① and ②). This is Hebrew for Eternal Light. The lamp symbolises the commandment to keep a light burning in the room where the Ark is kept, and is a reminder that God is always present.

Above the Ark you may also see a tablet or a plaque with Hebrew writing (picture ②). This plaque symbolises the **TEN COMMANDMENTS**, which are some of the most important parts of the Torah. The Hebrew writing on the plaque gives the first few words of each of the ten commandments.

Clothing for the Torah

One way that Jews show their love and respect for God and for God's teachings is by 'dressing' the Torah scrolls in beautiful covers and decorations (picture ③).

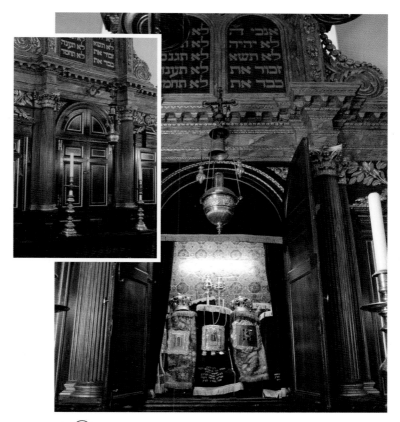

▲ ② The Ark always has doors and an inner curtain, called a parochet. This is because the Temple also had doors and curtains. During certain prayers, the doors and/or curtain are opened *(main picture)* or closed *(inset)*. This is done by a member of the congregation and is considered an honour.

▶ ③ The cloth covering on the scrolls is called the mantle. It is a reminder of the clothes the priests in the Temple used to wear. The silver plate is a reminder of the breastplate the high priest of the Temple wore. The crown on top of the scrolls is a reminder of the hat the high priest wore and the bells are a reminder of how the high priest had bells sown on his robe, so that everyone could hear him as he worshipped.

The sanctuary

The Torah and Ark are kept in a room called the sanctuary.

Inside every synagogue is a room used for prayer, called the **SANCTUARY**. This is where you can find the Torah scrolls and the Ark. In the sanctuary, all of the chairs will be facing the Ark. The sanctuary also contains many other things used in worship.

There is usually a raised platform in the sanctuary, called a **BIMAH** (picture ①). This is where the Torah scrolls are placed when they are read out loud during worship. It is also used as a raised platform for leading services.

◀ ① **An open Torah is lying on a bimah, ready to be read. You can see other Torah scrolls in the open Ark.**

Symbols of Judaism

There will also be a candelabrum with seven 'branches', called a **MENORAH** (picture ②). The menorah is a symbol of Judaism and reminds Jews of the commandment to "be a light unto nations".

▲ ② **The menorah in a stained glass window.**

Each branch stands for one of the days of the week, and reminds worshippers that God created everything in seven days.

There may also be a symbol called a **STAR OF DAVID** or, in Hebrew, *Magen David* (picture ③). This is a symbol of Judaism and a reminder of an ancient Jewish king called King David.

▲ ③ **The Star of David in stained glass.**

In some synagogues there may be art, such as stained glass, inside the sanctuary. Jews believe it is wrong to worship images of God, so the art in the synagogue will never show images of God.

Prayer books

Inside the sanctuary you will also find prayer books, called **SIDDUR** (picture ④). The siddur contain all of the prayers said during worship. There may also be copies of another book, called the chumash. The chumash is a book version of the Torah, so worshippers can follow along when the Torah scrolls are being read out loud.

▲ ④ **A prayer book, called the siddur.**

Sometimes the chumash also has an English translation of the Torah and writings about what the Torah means.

Because many Jews believe that they are not supposed to do any work between sundown Friday and sundown Saturday, the prayer books are usually kept in the sanctuary so people do not have to do the work of carrying them to the synagogue.

Clothing for worship

Many Jews wear special clothing when they worship.

◄ ① **Boys and men wear a kippah, or skullcap, during worship.**

When Jews come to the synagogue to worship, they usually dress in their best clothes, to show their respect. However, there are also some special clothes that Jews wear to worship which have an important meaning in Judaism.

Head covering

Most Jews believe that they should cover their head during worship. This is a sign of respect for God and is also a reminder that God is always present. Most Jewish men cover their heads during worship by wearing a kind of cap called a **KIPPAH**, or a skullcap (picture ①).

Kippah

Tallit

Tzitzit

► ② **There are many different customs about who should wear a tallit. In some communities only men wear the tallit, while in others both men and women wear them. Some people wear their tallit like a shawl, some wear it like a cloak, and still others wear it draped around their neck like a scarf.**

Many Jewish women also cover their heads by wearing a hat or a scarf.

Shawl and fringes

Many Jews believe that one of the commandments in the Torah is to wear fringes in the corners of their clothing during morning prayers or when reading the Torah.

However, clothing with corners was very common in ancient Israel, but is not common any more. So, in order to fulfil this commandment, some adult men wear a four-cornered shawl called a **TALLIT** to services (picture ②). Tied through a small hole in each corner of this shawl are the knotted fringes, called **TZITZIT** (pictures ② and ③).

Most tallit have a thicker piece of material sewn on to form a collar, which is often decorated with the words of the blessing that people say as they put the tallit on. Many tallit are also decorated with blue stripes.

Prayer boxes

The Torah also commands Jews to "hold fast to the commandments as a sign upon your hand and let them be as reminders before your eyes". So, while they are praying, some Jewish men wear two small boxes called **TEFILLIN**.

▼ ③ Fringes, called tzitzit, on the end of a tallit.

Each box has four prayers written inside it. One box is strapped to the left arm ("sign upon your hand") and the other box is worn on the head ("before your eyes").

A daily house of worship

In some synagogues, there is worship three times each day.

▲ ① A worshipper leads afternoon prayer in a synagogue.

Jews can pray alone and at any time, but most Jews believe that it is best to worship in a group.

According to Jewish tradition, group worship in the synagogue should take place three times each day – in the morning, afternoon and evening. However, in some synagogues, especially if they are very small, there may only be group worship a few times a week.

Shabbat

In every synagogue, there are special worship services on Friday nights and Saturday mornings. The time between sundown on Friday and sundown on Saturday is called **SHABBAT**, or the Sabbath. This is the Jewish day of rest.

Who leads worship?

Any adult who knows how, can lead worship (picture ①), but in most synagogues, the **RABBI** leads services (picture ②).

The word rabbi means teacher and the rabbi is a man or woman who has been specially trained to lead worship and to teach about the Torah and about Jewish traditions and customs.

The rabbi also officiates at weddings and funerals, and answers any questions that people may have about Judaism or Jewish worship.

Daily worship

Whenever it happens, every service has a set pattern. At each morning service, for example, the same prayers will be said in the same order – very little will change from day to day or from week to week.

Prayers and blessings

Daily worship services usually include a prayer called the **SHEMA**, and another prayer called the Amidah (picture ③). Some parts of the prayers are recited out loud and other parts are said silently by each worshipper.

On Shabbat there is a special service, which we will learn about on the following pages.

◀ ② A rabbi leads a worship service.

▼ ③ A prayer book, or siddur, opened to the page containing the Amidah prayer.

Weblink: www.CurriculumVisions.com

Shabbat and the Torah

On Shabbat there is a special worship service.

During Shabbat services, and on some special days throughout the year, parts of the Torah are read out loud. This is a very important part of worship in the synagogue.

Removing the Torah

The Torah is divided into sections and one section is read each week. So, over a year, the entire Torah is read in the synagogue.

When it is time to read from the Torah, the doors and curtain of the Ark are opened and the scrolls are removed from it. The scrolls are held up so that everyone can see them. They may also be paraded around the room, to let everyone get a closer look.

Then the scrolls are carefully 'undressed' (picture ①) and put on the bimah. The scrolls are then unrolled to the part that is going to be read. A special blessing is also said.

▲ ① 'Undressing' the Torah scroll during Shabbat services.

Reading from the Torah

Members of the congregation then come up to read parts of the Torah out loud (picture ②).

Anyone who is over 13 can read from the Torah, but it is a special honour to be chosen to read.

However, it is not easy to read the Torah and takes a lot of practice. This is because the Torah scrolls are always read in Hebrew during worship. Also, during worship the Torah is usually chanted in a special way. So, before anyone can read from the Torah during a worship service, they must learn how to do it.

Because the oils on your hand can damage the delicate scrolls, the person reading uses a pointer, called a *yad*, to keep their place (picture ③). *Yad* is the Hebrew word for hand.

After the Torah is read, the scrolls are 'dressed': put back in the Ark with the same care they were taken out.

Book of Prophets

Jews believe that in ancient times, some people were given messages from God. These people are called **PROPHETS** and their writings are called the **BOOK OF PROPHETS**. So, after the Torah scrolls are read, a section from the Book of Prophets is also read which helps explain the Torah reading.

On Shabbat, the rabbi may also give a sermon about anything he or she thinks is important.

▲ ② **Reading from the Torah scroll during worship.**

▼ ③ **The person reading the Torah scroll uses a *yad* to keep their place without damaging the scroll.**

A house of learning

One very important function of a synagogue is to provide a place for learning and study.

▼ ① There are lots of ways of learning in the synagogue. Young children may learn about the Torah through art.

Studying the Torah and other Jewish religious books is an important part of being Jewish. In fact, one of the commandments in the Torah is to learn about and teach the Torah.

Another commandment tells Jews to study religious scholars, and a third commandment says to honour the old and the wise. So, you can see that studying and learning throughout life are important parts of being Jewish.

Because it is often easier to study if you are doing it with other people, most synagogues have classes and educational programmes for people of all ages (picture ①).

Education in the synagogue may begin by teaching young children all about Jewish holidays and how and when to say different prayers and blessings (see page 22).

▲▼ ② Hebrew uses a different alphabet than English. The Hebrew alphabet has 22 letters. There are no lower case letters in Hebrew, all the letters are capitals. Hebrew writing starts at the right hand end of the line and reads towards the left. All the letters in the Hebrew alphabet are consonants. The vowel sounds are shown by putting little dots or dashes above or below the letters. These vowel signs are called *nikkudim.*

Learning Hebrew and the Torah

Because the Torah is written in Hebrew, learning the Hebrew language is an important part of Jewish religious education (picture ②). There are regular Hebrew classes for children in most synagogues.

Learning Jewish teachings

Many Jewish people also believe that it is not enough to be able to read the Torah, they must also think about what the Torah means and discuss it with others. So, many synagogues will also have classes and lectures in Torah study for all ages.

Weblink: www.CurriculumVisions.com

Celebrations and festivals

The synagogue is a place where the Jewish community comes to celebrate Jewish holidays and events.

There are many Jewish holidays and festivals throughout the year. Many of the Jewish holidays and festivals recall important stories in the Torah.

For example, Passover (*Pesach*, in Hebrew) recalls the time when God rescued the Jews from slavery in Egypt.

Sukkot is a harvest festival, but it is also a reminder of how the Jews camped in the desert after they left Egypt.

Hanukkah recalls the capture of the Temple in Jerusalem from Jewish enemies, and **PURIM** commemorates a time thousands of years ago when Jewish people living in Persia were saved from death by a Jewish woman called Esther.

New Year

Another important holiday that is celebrated in the synagogue is called **ROSH HASHANAH**, which means New Year. During Rosh Hashanah Jews think about any mistakes they have made in the past year and how they can be a better person in the next year. In the synagogue there are special services, and a ram's horn, called a shofar (shown top left), is blown like a trumpet. Everyone wishes each other *L'shanah tovah* (this is a Hebrew saying which means "for a good year") and gives gifts of sweets, for a sweet new year.

Each holiday is celebrated in different ways in the synagogue. For example, during Purim there are special services where the part of the Jewish Bible that tells the story of Purim is read from a separate scroll. Everyone wears costumes to synagogue and after the service there may be a carnival or fete.

Personal celebrations

Important days in people's lives are also celebrated at the synagogue, for example, marriage and birth.

One personal day which is usually celebrated in the synagogue is when a child turns 13. This is the age when a child can begin to be called up to read the Torah during service and is responsible for their religious actions, for example, not breaking any of the Jewish commandments.

A special ceremony is held where the child comes up to read a part of the Torah during service for the first time (picture ①). The child may also make a speech during the service. This celebration is called a **BAR MITZVAH** (son of the commandments) for boys and a **BAT MITZVAH** (daughter of the commandments) for girls.

▼ ① In this synagogue, a brother and sister are celebrating their Bar and Bat Mitzvah at the same time – they are twins. This is the first time they have read from the Torah during Shabbat services.

A house of gathering

The synagogue is the centre of the Jewish community.

The synagogue is called the house of gathering because it is the centre of the entire Jewish community and not only a place for prayer and worship.

Meeting others

One of the purposes of a synagogue is to provide a place to meet other Jewish people. In many synagogues there are weekly meetings and events that give people a chance to meet others with similar interests.

Many synagogues organise youth clubs, and women's and men's clubs, as another way to help people meet and make friends.

There may also be events at the synagogue, such as lectures, film screenings and bridge clubs, which are not about religion, but help to build a community.

After Friday night service it is traditional to have a meal with family members (picture ①). This is called the *oneg Shabbat* (the joy of Shabbat). Some synagogues have the Shabbat meal for anyone who would like to come.

▼ ① **These young children are practising having a Shabbat meal.**

A weekly timetable for a synagogue

Monday
6.30 a.m.	Morning services
3–4 p.m.	Learning to read Hebrew
7.30 p.m.	Evening services

Tuesday
6.30 a.m.	Morning services
4–5 p.m.	After school activity club for girls and boys aged 8–16
7.30 p.m.	Evening services
8–9.15 p.m.	Evening Torah study for beginners Continuing study of the Torah, class is currently discussing the book of Exodus.

Wednesday
6.30 a.m.	Morning services
1.00 p.m.	Afternoon services
1.30–3 p.m.	Seniors group
3–4 p.m.	Mummy (or Daddy) and me. Bring your baby and meet other new or expectant parents for socialising and discussions.
7.30 p.m.	Evening services
7.45 p.m.	Bi-weekly prayer meeting 1st and 3rd Wednesday of each month.

Thursday
6.30 a.m.	Morning services
7.30 p.m.	Evening services
8–9 p.m.	Tzedakah (charity) meeting. Meet to plan ways of raising money for charities around the world.

Friday
6.30 a.m.	Morning services
6–7 p.m.	Holiday committee. This week, plans for the synagogue fete to celebrate the upcoming holiday of Purim.
7.30 p.m.	Shabbat evening service
7.30–8.30 p.m.	Weekly Shabbat School, for children aged 6–13. After Shabbat School children will be walked to the sanctuary for the sermon and family worship.
8.30 p.m.	Shabbat sermon and family worship service
9.00 p.m.	Shabbat meal

Saturday
10.30 a.m.	Torah Service Worship service and Torah reading.
11–12 p.m.	Shabbat School for children aged 0–12
5–6 p.m.	1st and 3rd Saturday of each month, learn Israeli folk dancing (all levels welcomed)

Sunday
6.30 a.m.	Morning services
11–12.30 p.m.	How to be an educated congregant? Learn answers to all your questions.
11–12.30 p.m.	Mitzvah preparation for children aged 11–13
7.30 p.m.	Evening services

Giving to charity

Several of the commandments in the Torah tell Jews that they must give to charity. So, many synagogues function as social welfare agencies, collecting and giving out money for the poor and needy in their community. The Hebrew word for giving charity is **TZEDAKAH**.

Many synagogues also raise money to help people around the world (picture ②).

◄▼ ② **Making coloured rice jars to raise money for charity at a synagogue fete.**

Learning about Israel

The modern country of Israel was founded in 1948 as a homeland for Jews all over the world, and Jews from all over the world have become citizens of Israel. For this reason, many Jews who do not live in Israel are very interested in what happens there. So, many synagogues have talks and lectures about Israel and organise trips to Israel to visit important Jewish historical sites.

Index

Amidah 15
Ark 2, 3, 7, 9, 10, 16, 17

Bar/Bat Mitzvah 2, 20–21
bimah 2, 7, 10, 16
Book of Prophets 2, 17

celebrations 5, 20–21
charity 23
chumash 11
commandments 2, 7, 8, 9, 11, 13, 18, 20, 23

'dressing' Torah scroll 9, 17

education 5, 18–19

festivals 20
fringes 13

gathering, house of 5, 22–23
God 4, 5, 6, 7, 8, 9, 11, 12, 17, 20

Hanukkah 20
Hebrew 2, 4, 5, 6, 7, 9, 11, 16, 19, 20, 23
holidays 18, 20
Holocaust 2, 6

Israel 2, 4, 13, 23

Jerusalem 6, 20
Jew/Jewish people 2, 4 *and throughout*

Judaism 2, 4 *and throughout*

King David 11
King Solomon 6
kippah 2, 12

learning, house of 5, 18–19

Magen David 11
menorah 2, 7, 11
mezuzah 2, 6–7
mitzvah 2, 7, 20–21

ner tamid 2, 7, 9
New Year 20
nikkudim 19

parchment 2, 7, 8
parochet 9
Passover 20
plaque 6, 9
prayer 4, 5, 7, 9, 10, 11, 13, 14, 15, 18
prayer, house of 4, 5, 10
prayer book 11, 15
prayer box 6–7, 13
prayer shawl. *See* tallit
"promised land". *See* Israel
prophet 2, 17
Purim 2, 20

rabbi 2, 14–15, 17
Rosh Hashanah 2, 20

Sabbath. *See* Shabbat
sanctuary 2, 7, 10–11
Shabbat 2, 14, 15, 16–17, 21, 22
Shabbat meal 22
shaddai 7
Shema 2, 7, 15
'shin' 6–7
shofar 20
siddur 2, 11, 15
skullcap 12
stained glass 11
Star of David 2, 7, 11
Sukkot 20
synagogue 2, 4 *and throughout*

tallit 2, 12, 13
tefillin 2, 13
ten commandments 2, 7, 9
the Temple 2, 6, 9, 20
timetable for a synagogue 23
Torah 2, 7, 8–9, 10, 11, 13, 15, 16–17, 18, 19, 20–21, 23
Torah scroll 8–9, 10, 11, 16–17, 20
tzedakah 2, 23
tzitzit 2, 12, 13

'undressing' Torah scroll 9, 17

World War II 6

yad 16, 17

Curriculum Visions

Curriculum Visions is a registered trademark of Atlantic Europe Publishing Company Ltd.

Atlantic Europe Publishing

Teacher's Guide
There is a Teacher's Guide to accompany this book, available only from the publisher.

Dedicated Web Site
There's more about other great Curriculum Visions packs and a wealth of supporting information available at our dedicated web site:
www.CurriculumVisions.com

First published in 2004 by
Atlantic Europe Publishing Company Ltd
Copyright © 2004
Atlantic Europe Publishing Company Ltd
Reprinted 2005

Authors
Lisa Magloff, MA and Brian Knapp, BSc, PhD
Religious Adviser
Valerie Boyd-Hellner
Art Director
Duncan McCrae, BSc
Editor
Gillian Gatehouse
Senior Designer
Adele Humphries, BA
Acknowledgements
The publishers would like to thank the following for their help and advice:
Bevis Marks Synagogue, Hendon Reform Synagogue.

Photographs
The Earthscape Editions photolibrary.
Illustrations
David Woodroffe
Designed and produced by
Earthscape Editions
Printed in China by
WKT Company Ltd

Jewish synagogue – *Curriculum Visions*
A CIP record for this book is available from the British Library

Paperback ISBN 1 86214 417 6
Hardback ISBN 1 86214 419 2

This product is manufactured from sustainable managed forests. For every tree cut down at least one more is planted.